KU-414-151

THE FUNNIEST JOKES

7 JOKES FOR YEAR OLDS

FOR HILARIOUS KIDS

Compiled by Amanda Li

Illustrated by Jane Eccles

MACMILLAN CHILDREN'S BOOKS

Published 2021 by Macmillan Children's Books
an imprint of Pan Macmillan
The Smithson, 6 Briset Street, London EC1M 5NR
EU representative: Macmillan Publishers Ireland Limited,
Mallard Lodge, Lansdowne Village, Dublin 4
Associated companies throughout the world
www.panmacmillan.com

ISBN 978-1-5290-6601-2

1 3 5 7 9 8 6 4 2

A CIP catalogue record for this book is available from the British Library.

Printed and bound by CPI Group (UK) Ltd, Croydon CR0 4YY
Compiled by Amanda Li
Design by Perfect Bound Ltd

What do you call a
cat with eight legs?

An octopuss.

What kind of dog
smells of onions?

A hot dog.

How do you start a jelly race?

'Get, set, go!'

How do you start a teddy race?

'Ready, teddy, go!'

How do you start an insect race?

'One, two, flea, go!'

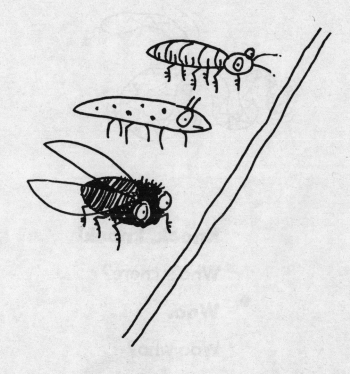

What vegetable do insects like?

Crawlieflower.

What hand should you use to pick up a poisonous snake?

Someone else's.

Knock, knock!

Who's there?

Woo.

Woo who?

Yes, I'm excited too!

What do bees like to chew?

Bumble gum.

What do you get if you cross a cat with a parrot?

A carrot.

What's a pirate's favourite
letter of the alphabet?

The 'C'.

What's a sailor's favourite biscuit?

Chocolate ship cookies.

What's the best
day for sailing?

Winds-day.

Why was Cinderella thrown
out of the football team?

**She ran away from
the ball.**

Why did the boy jump
around in the sink?

**He wanted to be
a tap dancer.**

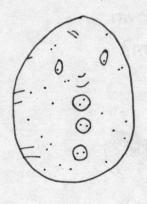

Customer: Waiter, there's a button in my salad!

Waiter: Sorry, it must have fallen off the jacket potato.

Why shouldn't you tell jokes when ice skating?

The ice might crack up.

What do you call a duck
who steals things from
bathrooms?

A robber duck.

Why do hummingbirds
hum?

**Because they don't
know the words.**

What did the cat say when it
ran out of money?

'I'm paw!'

What kind of animal can
jump higher than a house?

**Any kind. Houses
can't jump.**

Knock, knock!

Who's there?

Annie.

Annie who?

Annie way you can let me in?

What's a bat's favourite sport?

Batminton.

Knock, knock!

Who's there?

Cows say.

Cows says?

No – cows say 'Moo!'

What are rabbits'
favourite stories?

**Ones with hoppy
endings.**

What do you call a T-rex with
a banana in each ear?

**Anything you like -
it can't hear you.**

Why can't two waiters
play tennis?

**Because they both
want to serve.**

What did the big brother bug
say to the little brother bug?

**'Stop bugging
me!'**

What's the hardest
thing about learning
to ride a horse?

The ground.

If a monster runs through your front
door, what should you do?

Run out the back door.

Stan: I know how to make the school football team a lot better.

Coach: Great! So you're leaving it?

Dan: You've got holes in your shorts.

Stan: No, I don't!

Dan: Then how did you get your legs in them?

Stan: Coach said I could play in the school football team if it wasn't for two things.

Dan: What are they?

Stan: My feet.

What has 22 legs and goes 'Crunch, crunch!'

A football team eating crisps.

Why did the football quit the team?

It was tired of being kicked around.

Dan: Sorry, I missed that goal. I could kick myself!

Coach: Don't bother - you'd only miss.

Why did the
jelly wobble?

**It saw the
milk shake.**

Knock, knock!

Who's there?

Emma.

Emma who?

**Emma bit cold out here,
can you let me in?**

What vegetable should you
never take on a boat?

A leek.

Why did the chicken run
on to the football pitch?

**The referee called
a fowl.**

What's the best time
to buy a budgie?

**When they're
going 'Cheep'.**

Why would you never get
hungry on a desert island?

**Because of all the
sand which is there.**

What's small, crunchy and floats in space?

An astronut.

What do you call a skeleton that doesn't do any work?

Lazy bones.

Why can't two elephants go swimming?

Because they only have one pair of trunks.

What do you get if you cross a centipede and a parrot?

A walkie-talkie.

How does the Easter Bunny stay fit?

By doing lots of eggs-ercise.

What do frogs
eat with their
burgers?

French flies.

What do you call a sleepy
Stegosaurus?

A Stegosnore-us.

Where do bees
stop for the toilet?

At the BP station.

Knock, knock!

Who's there?

Justin.

Justin who?

**Justin time
for dinner!**

What did the fireman do with
his cat?

He put it out at night.

What has twelve legs, six eyes, three tails and can't see anything?

Three blind mice.

What do angry mice send each other at Christmas?

Cross mouse cards.

What do mice put
in their drinks?

Mice cubes.

What happened when the
cat ate a ball of wool?

She had mittens.

Why should you never play
football with a team of big cats?

They might be cheetahs.

What's a monkey's
favourite snack?

Chocolate chimp cookies.

What's the most
dangerous type of star?

A shooting star.

How do trees get on the internet?

They log on.

Knock, knock!

Who's there?

Twit.

Twit who?

Did anyone else hear an owl?

What do frogs
like to drink?

Croaka-Cola.

Why is it easy to weigh a fish?

They have their own scales.

Why did the barber win
the race?

He knew a short cut.

Why do mice need oiling?

Because they squeak.

Why did the bear
have no shoes on?

**He wanted
bare feet.**

Why did the chicken say 'Meow!'

It was learning a foreign language.

Meow!

Knock, knock!

Who's there?

Hugo.

Hugo who?

Hugo outside and I'll come in!

What colour is a burp?

Burple.

Where did the hamster
go on holiday?

Hamsterdam.

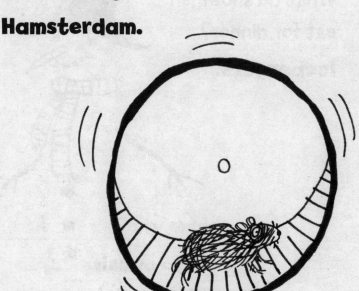

What's never hungry
at Christmas?

**The turkey – it's
always stuffed.**

What do snowmen
eat for dinner?

Icebergers.

What do skunks sing
at Christmas?

'Jingle Smells'.

What do snowmen like to
put on their icebergers?

Chilly sauce.

brrr!

chilly
sauce

What do you call
a deer in the rain?

A rain deer.

What do you get if
you cross a snowman
with a dog?

Frostbite.

What does a snowman
wear on its head?

An ice cap.

Why are snowmen
never brave?

**They always
get cold
feet.**

Where do snowmen
keep their money?

In a snow bank.

Why did the turkey join a band?

Because it had two drumsticks.

What do you get if you cross Santa with a duck?

A Christmas quacker.

What do elves do
after school?

Gnome-work.

What kind of bills do
elves have to pay?

Jingle bills.

What do baby elves
learn?

The elf-abet.

Millie: Did you hear the one about the three reindeer?

Tillie: No.

Millie: Dear, dear, dear!

Why is a turkey like an elf?

It's always a-gobblin'.

What do elves eat
at parties?

Fairy cakes.

What do you call a
snowman in the desert?

A puddle.

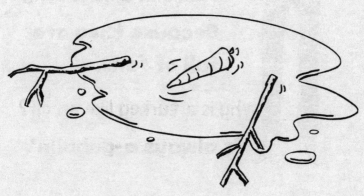

What's green and white
and bounces?

A spring onion.

Why are football
stadiums always cold?

**Because they are
full of fans.**

What's the most expensive
kind of fish?

A goldfish.

Knock, knock!

Who's there?

Amy.

Amy who?

Amy fraid I've forgotten!

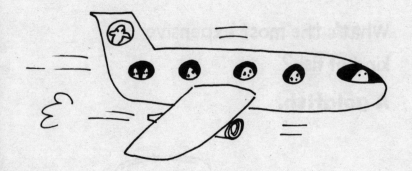

How do ghosts travel around?

By scareplane.

What goes 'Cackle, cackle, bonk!'

A witch laughing her head off.

Where do ghosts go swimming?

In the Dead Sea.

What's a ghost's
favourite country?

Wails.

How do you make
a witch itch?

**Take away
the 'W'.**

What do you call a donkey
with three legs?

A wonkey.

How do snakes sign
their messages?

**'With love and
hisses'.**

What do cats play at
birthday parties?

Puss the parcel.

What do cats read
in the morning?

Mewspapers.

What do cats wear
in bed?

Paw-jamas.

47

Why don't dogs drive cars?

They can never find a barking space.

What do you get if you cross a cat with a chocolate bar?

A Kitty-Kat.

What kind of stories
do cats like?

Furry tales.

Knock, knock!

Who's there?

Archie.

Archie who?

Bless you!

49

What do you call two bananas?

A pair of slippers.

What did the hat say to the scarf?

'You hang around and I'll go on ahead!'

Knock, knock!

Who's there?

Police.

Police who?

Police open the door!

What's a sea monster's
favourite dinner?

Fish and ships.

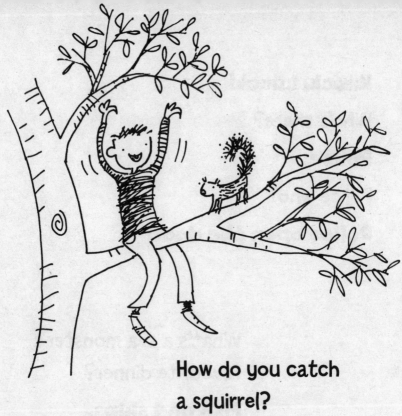

How do you catch
a squirrel?

**Climb up a tree
and act like a nut.**

What kind of room
doesn't have doors?

A mushroom.

Why was the nose tired?

Because it was always running.

Why did the cucumber need help?

It was in a pickle.

Why did the strawberry call for help?

It was in a jam.

How do you know when it's raining
cats and dogs?

**When you step
in a poodle.**

What kind of tie
does a pig wear?

A pigs-ty.

What do you give
a sick pig?

Oinkment.

Knock, knock!

Who's there?

Radio.

Radio who?

**Radio not,
here I come!**

What kind of fish
only swims at night?

A starfish.

How do you talk to
a giant?

Use very BIG words.

What's wobbly and flies?

A jelly-copter.

What do you call a girl
who stands between
the goalposts?

Annette.

Where do bees meet
to go into town?

At the buzz stop.

Knock, knock!

Who's there?

Tank.

Tank who?

You're welcome!

Why was the snake good at maths?

Because he was an adder.

Why should you never
tell Humpty Dumpty
a joke?

He might crack up.

What sort of glasses
do ghosts wear?

Spooktacles.

What should you
give a sick bird?

Tweetment.

What do you call a
worm in a fur coat?

A caterpillar.

What's brown, hairy
and wears sunglasses?

**A coconut on
holiday.**

What kind of tree
fits in your hand?

A palm tree.

Did you hear the joke about
the egg?

**Never mind, it was
rotten anyway.**

Which dog likes having
its hair washed?

A shampoodle.

What's a cow's
favourite day?

Moo Year's Day.

Knock, knock!

Who's there?

Rabbit.

Rabbit who?

Rabbit up nicely, it's a present!

What do sheep
do in the summer?

Go to baa-baa-cues.

Which hand is better
to write with?

**Neither. It's better
to write with a pen.**

What did the banana say
to the dog?

**Nothing.
Bananas
can't talk.**

What do you get if you cross
an alligator with a frog?

A croakadile.

Why did the car
stop in the road?

**It was wheely,
wheely tired.**

Did you hear the joke about
the bed?

It hasn't been made yet.

What do you get if you pour
hot water down a rabbit hole?

Hot cross bunnies.

Knock, knock!

Who's there?

Harry.

Harry who?

**Harry up and
answer the door!**

What do you call a
dinosaur who keeps
you awake at night?

A dinosnore.

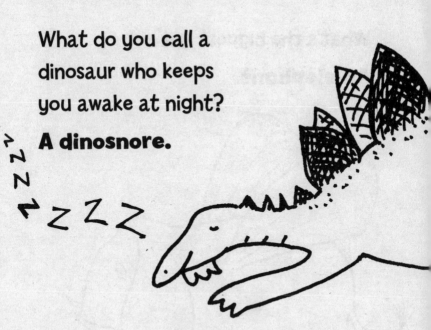

Why do hens
lay eggs?

**Because if they
threw them,
they would break.**

What's the biggest ant?

An elephant.

What did the policeman
say to his tummy?

'You're under a vest!'

Knock, knock!

Who's there?

Witches.

Witches who?

**Witches
the way
home,
please?**

What do you call a boomerang
that doesn't come back?

A stick.

What goes 'Zzub, zzub!'

A bee flying backwards.

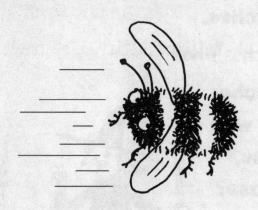

What time is it when a lion enters the room?

Time to leave.

Millie: My new shoes hurt.

Billy: That's because you've got them on the wrong feet.

Millie: But they're the only feet I've got.

woof!

How do you stop a dog from barking in the house?

Put it in the garden.

Why did the boy put sugar
under his pillow?

**He wanted to have
sweet dreams.**

What kind of witch
lives in the desert?

A sandwich.

How do you make an
octopus laugh?

With ten tickles.

How can you tell
one cat from
another?

**Look them
up in a
catalogue.**

What do astronauts spread
on their toast?

Mars-malade.

Knock, knock!

Who's there?

Boo!

Boo who?

**Don't cry,
it's only a joke!**

What's black and white and goes round and round?

A zebra in a revolving door.

What do you call a sheep
with no legs or head?

A cloud.

What's green and can jump
a mile a minute?

A grasshopper with hiccups.

What do you do when
a pig gets sick?

Call a hambulance.

Why do giraffes
have really long
necks?

**Because their
feet smell.**

Why do porcupines
win at games?

**They always have
the most points.**

Knock, knock!

Who's there?

Lettuce.

Lettuce who?

Lettuce in, it's cold out here!

What do you call a bee
who's always complaining?

A grumble bee.

Why do all witches look the same?

**So you can't tell which witch
is which.**

What do cats eat
for breakfast?

Mice Krispies.

What sound do hedgehogs
make when they kiss?

'Ouch!'

How would a frog feel
if it broke its leg?

Unhoppy.

What do you call a bear in the rain?
A drizzly bear.

What do you get if
you walk under a cow?
A pat on the head.

What do you give a seasick monster?
Lots of room.

Knock, knock!

Who's there?

Doris.

Doris who?

Doris locked, that's why we're knocking!

Who brings elephants their Christmas presents?

Elephanta Claus.

What do elephants do after school?

Watch ele-vision.

What's big, grey and red?

An elephant with sunburn.

How do you know if there's
an elephant in your fridge?

You can't shut the door.

What's big, grey and
wears glass slippers?

A Cinderellaphant!

What do you call
an elephant at the
North Pole?

Lost.

What do you do if an
elephant sits on your fence?

Get a new fence.

Why are leopards no good
at playing hide-and-seek?

They are always spotted.

Why are fish so clever?

They live in schools.

What do you
call a pig that
does karate?

A pork chop.

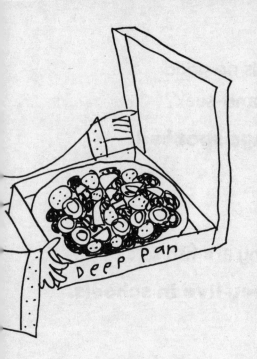

Knock, knock!

Who's there?

Handsome.

Handsome who?

Handsome pizza to me, please!

What time is it when the clock strikes thirteen?

Time to get a new clock.

Why couldn't the car
play football?

It only had one boot.

How do ghosts like
their eggs cooked?

Terrifried.

What do you get if you cross a spaniel, a poodle and a cockerel?

A cocker-poodle-doo.

What do you call an angry puzzle?

A crossword.

Knock, knock!

Who's there?

Doughnut.

Doughnut who?

Doughnut ask silly questions!

What did the bowling ball
say to the bowling pins?

**'Out of the way,
I'm on a roll!'**

What do ghosts put
in their sandwiches?

Scream cheese.

How do baby lions cross
the road?

**They wait until they
see a zebra crossing.**

What do birds do
at Halloween?

Trick or tweet.

What music do Egyptian
mummies like best?

Wrap.

What fur do we get
from a grizzly bear?

As fur away as possible.

What do mice do when they're at home?

Mousework.

Knock, knock!

Who's there?

Leaf.

Leaf who?

Leaf me alone!

Where do hamburgers
go to dance?
Meatballs.

What do you get if
you cross a kangaroo
with a sheep?
**A woolly
jumper.**

What do you call a bee
that can't make up
his mind?

A maybe.

What has four wheels and flies?

A rubbish truck.

Why should you never
trust stairs?

**They're always up
to something.**

What do you get if you
cross a skunk with a
dinosaur?

A stinkosaurus.

What's worse than a giraffe
with a sore throat?

A centipede with blisters.

Maths teacher: If I had twenty bananas in one hand and thirty bananas in the other, what would I have?

Pupil: Massive hands!

What's the best thing to put into a pie?

Your teeth.

Knock, knock!

Who's there?

Hippo.

Hippo who?

Hippo Birthday to you!

Where do frogs put
their coats?

In the croakroom.

Have you heard the joke about the wall?

I'd tell you but you'd never get over it.

What do you call a
deer with no eyes?

No-eye-deer.

What do you get when a
skunk plays table tennis?

Ping pong.

What do you call a
monkey with a wand?

Hairy Potter.

What's yellow, brown and hairy?

**Cheese on toast dropped
on the carpet.**

Knock, knock!

Who's there?

Hugo.

Hugo who?

Hugo first, I'm scared!

What do ghosts like best at theme parks?

The roller-ghoster.

Why don't skeletons
go to discos?

**They have nobody
to dance with.**

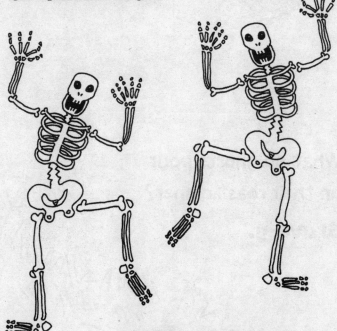

What's a skeleton's
favourite musical
instrument?

A trombone.

How do squirrels do online shopping?

On the internut.

What do ghosts pour on their roast dinner?

Grave-y.

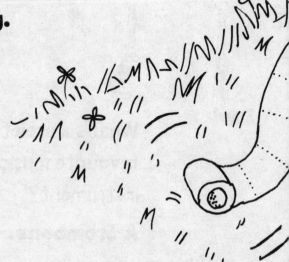

How do baby
bees travel?

By minibuzz.

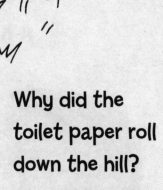

Why did the
toilet paper roll
down the hill?

**To get to the
bottom.**

Knock, knock!

Who's there?

Eddie.

Eddie who?

Eddie body home?

Which animal is
always laughing?

A happy-potamus.

What kind of pet
did Aladdin have?

A flying carpet.

What's the
noisiest pet?

A trumpet.

What do you get if you cross a
cow with a grass cutter?

A lawn-mooer.

What kind of tea do
footballers drink?

Penaltea.

What day do fish hate?

Fry-day.

What do snakes
learn at school?

Hisss-tory.

How do hedgehogs
play leapfrog?

Very carefully.

Why did the fly fly?

Because the spider spied 'er.

Knock, knock!

Who's there?

Dishes.

Dishes who?

Dishes a very bad joke!

What do you call a sick crocodile?

An illigator.

When is it unlucky to see
a black cat?

**When you're
a mouse.**

23, 24, 25, 26...

How do you count cows?

With a cowculator.

Where do cows go on
a Saturday night?

To the moo-vies.

How do you make a milkshake?

Creep up behind a glass of milk and shout 'BOO!'

In which season should you get a trampoline?

Spring.

Why did the banana go to the doctor?

It wasn't peeling well.

Why does a flamingo lift one leg up?

Because if it lifted two legs, it would fall over.

Knock, knock!

Who's there?

Scott.

Scott who?

Scott nothing to do with you!

What's a ghost's favourite day of the week?

Moan-day.

What did dinosaurs
have that no other
animals have?

Baby dinosaurs.

What do you call a
person who steals cows?

A beefburglar.

Why did the boy take a pencil
to bed?

**He wanted to draw the
curtains.**

Millie: Is the school cook
any good?

Billy: Well – yesterday the
salad was burnt.

Where do ghosts buy stamps?

At the ghost office.

What do you call
a fairy that hasn't
washed?

Stinkerbell.

Knock, knock!

Who's there?

Oscar.

Oscar who?

Oscar silly question, get a silly answer!

What's a frog's favourite sweet?

A lolli-hop.

Why do aliens never
go hungry in space?

**Because they know where
to find a Galaxy, a Mars
and a Milky Way.**

How do you get a
baby astronaut
to sleep?

Rock-et.

How do snails get ready for a party?

They put on snail varnish.

Dad: Jack, you *can't* keep
a pig in your bedroom.

Jack: Why not?

Dad: It smells terrible!

Jack: Don't worry,
he'll get used to it.

Knock, knock!

Who's there?

Owl.

Owl who?

Owl be very sad if you don't let me in!

What did the right football boot say to the left football boot?

'Between us, we should have a ball!'

What game do baby ghosts play?

Hide-and-eek.

What do you call a bull
in a washing machine?

Wash-a-bull.

Why did the lobster blush?

Because the sea weed!

Why did the man run
around his bed?

**He was trying to catch
up on his sleep.**

Why didn't the dog
want to play tennis?
It was a boxer.

How do you make a goldfish old?
Take away the 'G'.

What do you get if you cross a
football team with an ice-cream van?
Aston Vanilla.

Who delivers Christmas
presents to dogs?
Santa Paws.

PILLGWENLLY